YOUNG WOMEN'S EDITION
MUSICAL THEATRE ANTHOLOGY FOR TEENS

COMPILED BY LOUISE LERCH

infringement of copyright.

Visit Hal Leonard Online at
www.halleonard.com

CD CONTENTS

DISC ONE

DISC TWO

CONTENTS

Adelaide's Lament
from GUYS AND DOLLS

By FRANK LOESSER

As Long As He Needs Me

from the Columbia Pictures -
Romulus Motion Picture Production of Lionel Bart's OLIVER!

Words and Music by
LIONEL BART

A Bushel and a Peck
from GUYS AND DOLLS

By FRANK LOESSER

Light Bounce Tempo

Candle on the Water
from Walt Disney's PETE'S DRAGON

Words and Music by AL KASHA
and JOEL HIRSCHHORN

I'll be your can-dle on the wa-ter, my love for you will al-ways
I'll be your can-dle on the wa-ter 'til ev-'ry wave is warm and

burn. I know you're lost and drift-ing, but the clouds are lift-ing.
bright. My soul is there be-side you, let this can-dle guide you;

Don't give up; you have some-where to turn.
soon you'll see a gold-en stream of light.

Colors of the Wind
from Walt Disney's POCAHONTAS

Music by ALAN MENKEN
Lyrics by STEPHEN SCHWARTZ

think I'm an ig-no-rant sav-age, and you've been so man-y plac-es, I guess it must be so. But

still I can-not see, if the sav-age one is me, how can there be so much that you don't

Can You Feel the Love Tonight
from Walt Disney Pictures' THE LION KING

Music by ELTON JOHN
Lyrics by TIM RICE

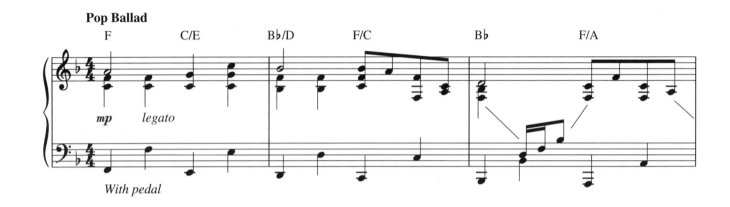

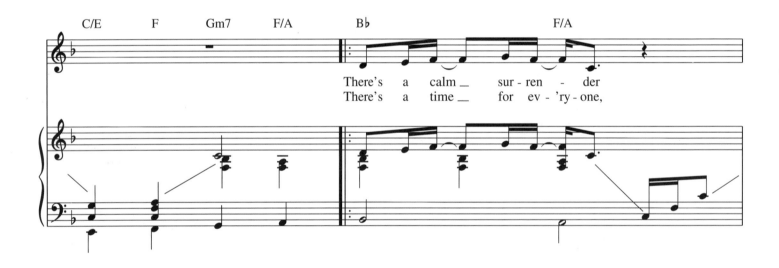

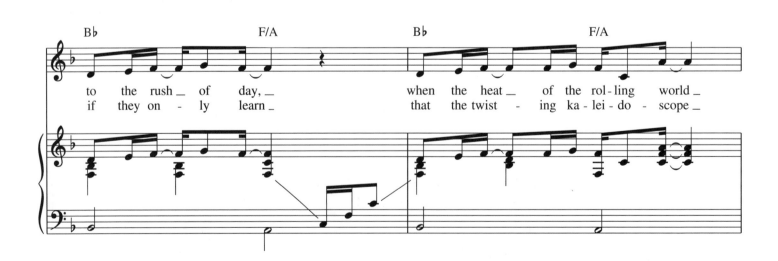

A Change in Me
from Walt Disney's BEAUTY AND THE BEAST:
THE BROADWAY MUSICAL

Music by ALAN MENKEN
Lyrics by TIM RICE

* Original Broadway key: Gb

No change of heart, a change in me. _____

A Cockeyed Optimist
from SOUTH PACIFIC

Lyrics by OSCAR HAMMERSTEIN II
Music by RICHARD RODGERS

Dance If It Makes You Happy
from THE TAP DANCE KID

Written by HENRY KRIEGER
and ROBERT LORICK

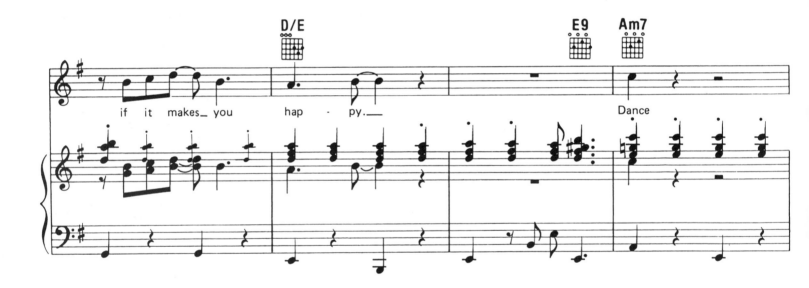

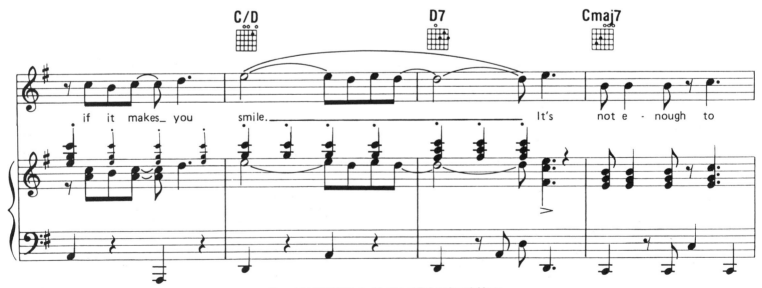

Disneyland
from SMILE

Words by HOWARD ASHMAN
Music by MARVIN HAMLISCH

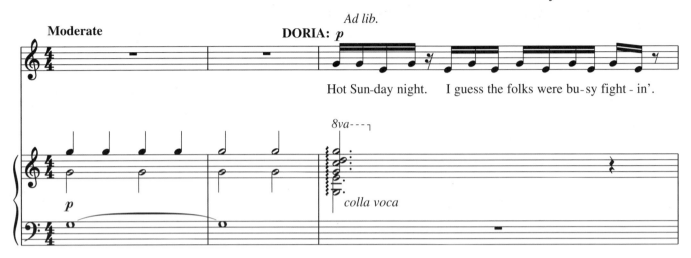

Dis - ney-land __ on a west - ern breeze, mag - ic car - pet,

please, car - ry me a - way __

__ Oh, I know you're gon-na say the trees are pa-per-mâc-hé, __ It's done with

solo

mp

mir - rors, the mag - ic there. __ Each lit - tle bird's full of springs, __ you press a but-ton, it sings, __ re-cord - ed

mp

mf

take me there _ to Dis - ney - land, _____

_ and when I get to Dis - ney - land

8vb - ⌟

I'll stay. _____

Slow

ff

tr

sf   p

Falling Out of Love Can Be Fun
from the Stage Production MISS LIBERTY

Words and Music by
IRVING BERLIN

Don't Call Me Trailer Trash
from COWGIRLS

Written by MARY MURFITT

Steadily

look at all them pic - tures in the mag - a - zines _____ where they
You can al - ways keep me down on the farm 'cause I've

show you all the mod - els in de - sign - er jeans.
al - ways liked a man with a half tan arm.

All the girls are skin - ny, and their hair is flat. Why would
pick - up truck with o - ver - sized tires Makes me

I want to look like that? I like the fash - ion don'ts
weak in the knees and sets my heart on fire. Cheese fries, wise guys,

____ and not the do's. I read the com - ics, and I
dem - o - li - tion der - by. Stir frys, nice guys

throw a - way the news. Cit - y folks laugh at my K - Mart clothes, but I
do noth - in' fer me. Nev - er cut out gour - met rec - i - pes, I pre -

Fabulous Feet
from THE TAP DANCE KID

Written by HENRY KRIEGER
and ROBERT LORICK

Moderate Swing, with a feel

I ain't got a shin-y black car.___ I ain't got a bun-dle of bright___ ___green mon-ey. The clothes on my back ___ are off the rack, but know what? So what! I don't care___ 'cause you

Goodnight, My Someone
from Meredith Willson's THE MUSIC MAN

By MEREDITH WILLSON

light for good-night, my love, for good-night. _____ Sweet

dreams be yours, dear, if dreams there be; Sweet dreams to

car - ry you close to me. I wish they may, and I

wish they might. Now good-night, my some - one, good - night. _____

Poco mosso

True love can be whis-pered from heart to heart, when lov-ers are part-ed they say. But I must de-pend on a wish and a star, as long as my heart does-n't know who you are. Sweet dreams be yours, dear, if dreams there

I Have Confidence
from THE SOUND OF MUSIC

Music and Lyrics by
RICHARD RODGERS

Moderato (rubato)

What will this day be like? I won-der. _ What will my fu-ture

Più mosso

be? I won-der. _ It could be so ex-cit-ing to be out in the world, to be

free. My heart should be wild-ly re-joic-ing. Oh, what's the mat-ter with

Con moto

I have con-fi-dence in sun - shine,____

I have con-fi-dence in rain.____ I have con - fi-dence that

spring will come a - gain. Be - sides which, you see, I have con - fi-dence in me.

Strength does - n't lie in num - bers,____ Strength does - n't lie in

wealth._____ Strength lies in nights of peace - ful slum - bers.

When you wake up, wake up!___ It's health - y. All I

trust I leave my heart to. _____ All I trust be - comes my

own. _____ I have con - fi - dence in con - fi - dence a -

rit. e dim.

I'll Know
from GUYS AND DOLLS

By FRANK LOESSER

Moderately

I'm Gonna Wash That Man Right Outa My Hair

from SOUTH PACIFIC

Lyrics by OSCAR HAMMERSTEIN II
Music by RICHARD RODGERS

I Won't Say
(I'm in Love)
from HERCULES

Music by ALAN MENKEN
Lyrics by DAVID ZIPPEL

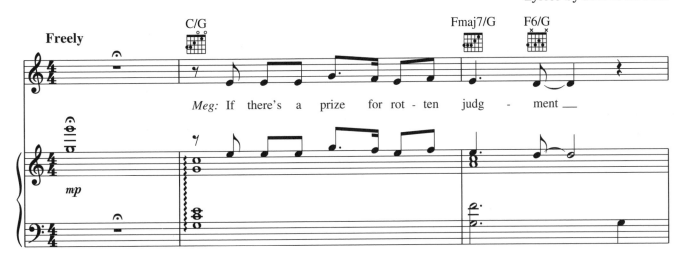

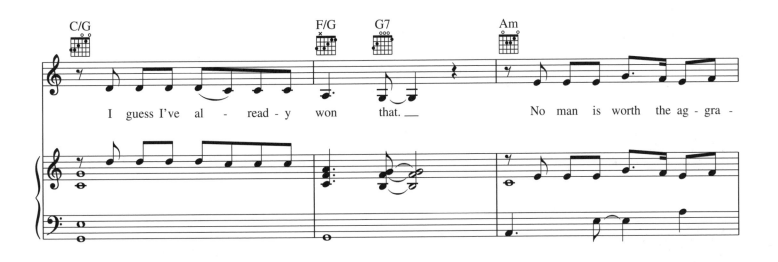

In My Life
from LES MISÉRABLES

Music by CLAUDE-MICHEL SCHÖNBERG
Lyrics by HERBERT KRETZMER
Original Text by ALAIN BOUBLIL and JEAN-MARC NATEL

It Might as Well Be Spring
from STATE FAIR

Lyrics by OSCAR HAMMERSTEIN II
Music by RICHARD RODGERS

I've Never Been in Love Before
from GUYS AND DOLLS

By FRANK LOESSER

Johnny One Note
from BABES IN ARMS

Words by LORENZ HART
Music by RICHARD RODGERS

Missing You (My Bill)
from THE CIVIL WAR: AN AMERICAN MUSICAL

Words by JACK MURPHY
Music by FRANK WILDHORN

Miss Marmelstein
from I CAN GET IT FOR YOU WHOLESALE

Words and Music by
HAROLD ROME

My New Philosophy
from YOU'RE A GOOD MAN, CHARLIE BROWN

Words and Music by
ANDREW LIPPA

SALLY: *Spoken (before the vamp): "Why are you telling me?" (beat) I like it.*

* *Original key: A Major*

The song is a duet for Sally and Schroeder. The composer created this solo edition for publication.

Nothing
from A CHORUS LINE

Words by EDWARD KLEBAN
Music by MARVIN HAMLISCH

Easy 2 - Rock feel

DIANA:

Spoken:

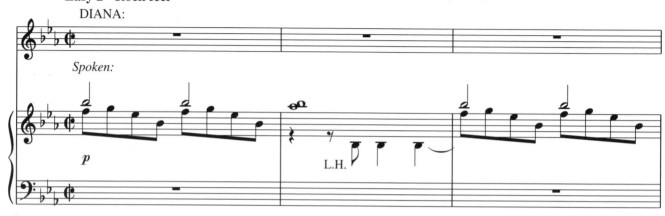

I mean, I was dying to be a serious actress. Anyway it's the first day of acting class and we're in the

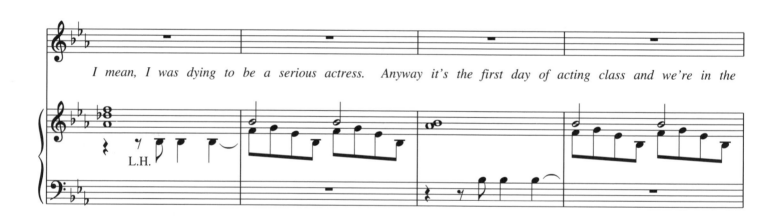

auditorium and the teacher, Mister Karp, puts us up on the stage with our legs around everybody, one in back of

down the hill. _____ Ev-'ry day for a week we would try to

hear the wind rush, hear the wind rush,

feel the chill. _____ And I dug right down to the bot-tom of my soul to see_

__ what I had in - side. _ Yes, I dug right down to the

bot-tom of my soul and I tried, _____ I tried.

Spoken: *Everyone is going:* *"Woosh... I feel the snow, I feel the cold...the air."* *And Mr. Karp*

turns to me and says: *"O.K. Morales, what did you feel?"* *Sung:* And I said, "Noth-ing, ___

Vamp under dialogue

I'm feel-ing noth-ing,"___ and he says, "Noth-ing ___ could

124

- les, ____ all a-lone." So I dug right down to the

bot-tom of my soul to see ____ how an ice cream felt. ____ Yes, I dug right down to the

bot-tom of my soul and I tried _____ to melt.

The kids yelled "Noth-ing!" ____ They called me

"Noth-ing!"_ And Karp al-lowed it, which real-ly makes me burn. They were so help-ful. They called me hope-less. Un-til I real-ly did-n't know where else to turn! *Spoken: And Karp kept saying:* "*Morales, I think you should transfer to girls' high.*

You'll never be an actress Never!" Jesus Christ!

Sung: Went to church pray-ing, "San - ta Ma - ri - a, send me guid - ance,

send me guid - ance." On my knees.

Went to church pray-ing, "San - ta Ma - ri - a, help me feel it,

Ad lib.

Six months lat-er I heard that Karp had died. _____

And I dug right down to the bot-tom of my soul....

Slowly

and cried, _____ 'cause I felt...

Tempo I

noth-ing. _____

Nothing Can Stop Me Now!

from THE ROAR OF THE GREASEPAINT – THE SMELL OF THE CROWD

Words and Music by LESLIE BRICUSSE
and ANTHONY NEWLEY

Once You Lose Your Heart
from ME AND MY GIRL

Words and Music by
NOEL GAY

Rubato, molto legato, cantabile

Once you lose your heart, Once some-bod-y takes it,

From the place it rest-ed in be-fore. Once you lose your heart,

Once some-bod-y wakes it, then it is-n't your heart an-y more. _____ It's

più mosso

say a girl should nev - er be with - out love, _____ And

all the joy that love a - lone can bring. All that I have ev - er learnt a -

bout love, _____ tells me it's a ver - y __ fun - ny thing. _____ For

when your heart is fan - cy - free, You hope some man will choose it, But

rall.

ev - er go that way, And now you must pur - sue it for - ev - er and a day.

rall. e dim.

Tempo Primo

Once you lose your heart, Once some-bod - y takes it, There's one thing cer-tain from the

poco accel.

rall.

start, _____ You've got to fol - low, You've got to

rall. al fine

f

fol - low your heart. _____

mp

dim.

8ba

Reflection
from Walt Disney Pictures' MULAN

Music by MATTHEW WILDER
Lyrics by DAVID ZIPPEL

Reflectively

MULAN: Look at me, I will nev-er pass ___ for a per-fect bride or a per-fect daugh-ter. Can it be I'm not meant to play this part? Now I see that if I were tru-ly to be my-self,

So Many People
from SATURDAY NIGHT

Music and Lyrics by
STEPHEN SONDHEIM

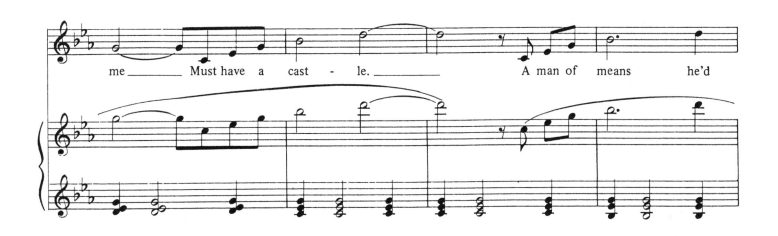

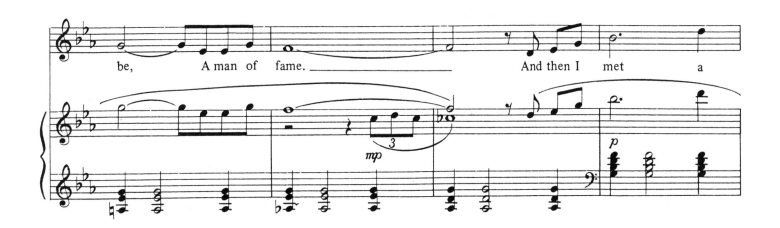

man _____ Who had-n't an - y, _____ With-out a pen - ny _____

_____ To his name. _____ I had to go and

fall _____ For so much less than _____ What I had

planned from all _____ the mag-a - zines. _____ I should be

good and sore: _____ What am I hap - py for? _____ I guess the

man means more _____ Than the means. _____

Non rubato (♩ = 48)

So man-y peo - ple in the world, And

what can they do? _____ They'll nev - er know love _____ Like

Shy
from ONCE UPON A MATTRESS

Words by MARSHALL BARER
Music by MARY RODGERS

Allegretto

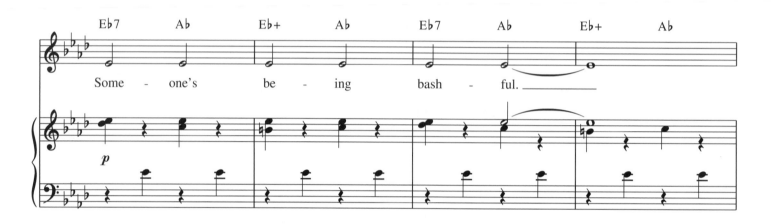

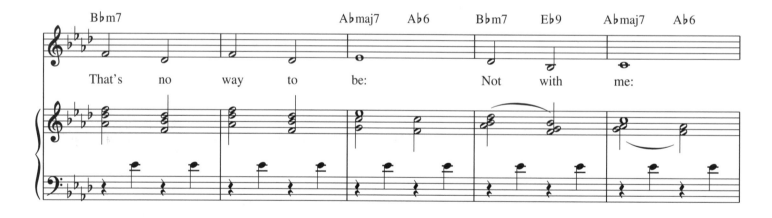

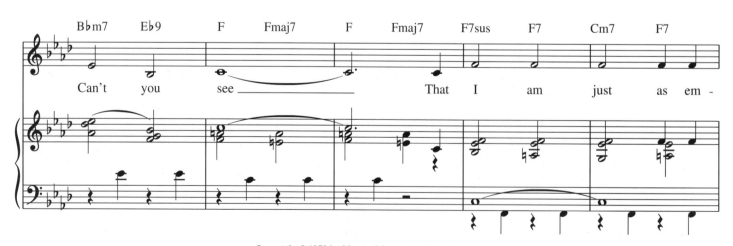

Someone Like You
from JEKYLL & HYDE

Lyrics by LESLIE BRICUSSE
Music by FRANK WILDHORN

Slowly, with expression

mp

I peered through win-dows, watched life go by. Dreamed of to-mor-row,
It's like you took my dreams, made each one real. You reached in-side of me

but stayed in-side. The past was hold-ing me,
and made me feel. And now I see a world

Violets and Silverbells
from SHENANDOAH

Words by PETER UDELL
Music by GARY GELD

Whistle Down the Wind
from WHISTLE DOWN THE WIND

Music by ANDREW LLOYD WEBBER
Lyrics by JIM STEINMAN

Wild and Reckless
from DRAT! THE CAT!

Lyric by IRA LEVIN
Music by MILTON SCHAFER